JESUS LOVES ME

Jesus Loves Me

R. Earl Allen

BROADMAN PRESS
Nashville, Tennessee

Dewey Decimal Classification: 232
Subject Heading: JESUS CHRIST

Library of Congress Catalog Card Number: 78-72846
Printed in the United States of America

Dedicated to
my brother, *James A. Allen,*
with love and appreciation

Contents

1 Because He Is Unchanging

> Jesus Christ the same yesterday, and to day, and for ever (Hebrews 13:8).

When we stand at the threshold of a New Year or at any other time of personal evaluation, we must look backwards as well as forwards. Just as merchants take time to inventory their stock, we need to inventory our successes and failures, our triumphs and tragedies. No merchant would try to take an inventory in the middle of a giant clearance sale. He would have to close the store to make a sensible estimate of his assets and liabilities. A sensible and sensitive Christian would also evaluate his assets and liabilities at leisure. Self-evaluation isn't something we can do on the run.

Perhaps the best spiritual preparation we can make for the future is a long, honest look at the past. We might ask ourselves, What have I achieved for Christ?

Have I grown in grace? Am I stronger in
the faith? Where do I stand in relation to
his divine will?

In order to ask these questions and answer them honestly, we will need to remove
ourselves from in front of the television set,
unplug the telephone, and shut out the in-
terruptions that daily crowd in and prevent
our spending time with ourselves.

One of the items that causes me to
reflect on the past is my minister's calendar.
For several years I have used one of these,
transferring certain dates from the previous
year onto the calendar of the new year. I
always note funerals, weddings, confer-
ences, special occasions. Sometimes, as I
look over the last year's calendar, I see days
that mark sad events in my life. My tears
and my joys are wrapped up in the pages
of that calendar.

Does change always mean progress,
or sometimes do we merely move, simply
blundering along? One fact is certain:
whether we make progress or not, we do
change. Physically, we change—that is ob-
vious. Spiritually, we ought to be changing
every day. Mentally, we ought to grow hour
by hour.

But we often find ourselves growing

used to the *status quo,* and then we must make a trip backward in time in order to see the difference. When we go back to an old familiar place, we see that neither we nor the place is the same; nothing is quite the way we remembered it. We see differences; we see depreciation. All around us we see change.

A familiar saying goes, "only change is constant," but that saying has one exception. Jesus Christ never changes. He need not, he cannot, he will not change. He is the same yesterday, today, and forever. Thank God for the stability of a Savior who is unchanging amid constant change! The greatest asset we have is the unchanging Christ within us, who loves us the same today as yesterday, regardless of the mistakes we have made.

Unchanged in Person

When we consider Jesus, we usually think of him as a babe in Bethlehem, or as a young boy puttering about his home. We recognize him as he comes to the Temple, works in the carpenter's shop, or selects his disciples by the sea. But Jesus of Bethlehem, Jesus of Nazareth did not originate in Judea. He was before the foundation of the world.

He existed in creation, one with God the Father and God the Holy Spirit. His person has not been changed.

The Same in the Present

Jesus Christ entered the world and became God-man. He lived as men lived, worked as men worked. Born into a working family, he labored always—in the carpentry shop and in his ministries. He worked with an urgency since he had come to "work the works of him who sent me." He asked working men to follow him, to lay down their fishing nets, and to fish for men.

Work was important to Jesus, and it should be important to us. We too have been called to labor in the fields. We are to work while it is day, for "the night cometh, when no man can work" (John 9:4). Christ is working today, in us and in the world, and we should do no less than strive to honor and glorify him.

Jesus is the same today as he was in Bethlehem—a pioneer! He is as mindful of the problems of the Supreme Court as he was of the problems of Pilate's Court. He is as aware of the temptations of drugs today as he was of the temptations of old. But he has promised, for our time as well as his own, that "there hath no temptation taken you but such as is common to man . . . but will with the temptation also make a way to escape" (1 Cor. 10:13). God is our God for today!

During one of the crucial days of battle, when Napoleon's soldiers were losing badly, the commander walked into the midst of his armies and said, "Men, your emperor is here." His presence changed the course of the battle, and his armies went on to victory. But as Napoleon neared the end of his life, he acknowledged, "In my prime I could get thousands to follow me, *but I had to be there.*"

Napoleon is no longer here, but Christ is! He has lived in us ever since the tombstone was rolled away. God has claimed victory over death and the grave and has promised to lead victoriously any who would follow him.

God is here, and he cares. He is God of the present—the same yesterday, TODAY, and forever, world without end, Amen.

The Same to His People

Unchanged in his Person, and unchanged in the present, Christ is also unchanged before his people.

Remember the dark day in the life of Mary and Martha, the day when Lazarus died? They wondered, as many of us do when the moment strikes, Why us? What have we done? One of the sisters was consoled by those who came to the home to visit; the other was unconsoled in her grief until the Master came.

God has not changed in his power to comfort. The Lord's presence is the only thing that really makes any difference. Jesus said to his disciples, "I will not leave you comfortless; I will come to you" (John 14:18).

God also has not changed in his promise of peace. The hymn calls it "sweet peace, the gift of God's love." You can get God's peace only as a gift of his love. "Peace I leave with you, my peace I give unto you," Jesus told the disciples (John 14:2). In those dark moments after the crucifixion and resurrection, he stood, with nail-scarred hands, before his apostles, promising peace to those who believed. That peace has not changed; Jesus is Peacegiver today as well as yesterday.

The best work a pastor does is always behind closed doors with aching hearts. I listened as a man cried out in repentance, his experience like that of so many. "Would you tell me how to become the man I once was? I have nothing now but disturbance, lack of sleep, heartache, and agony."

"You once had that peace?" I asked.

"Yes, there was a day when I knew the peace of God."

"When did you lose it?"

"When I started dropping out of church."

So many of us think the preacher is meddling when he knocks on the door to encourage attendance. But once a man has tasted the things of God, once he has had his thirst quenched by the living water, he cannot go back to the stagnant waters of the world. Any time a man leaves God's house, His Word, and His people, and goes his own way, he damages his conscience and his peace as well. "They went out from us, but they were not of us, for if they had been of us, they would no doubt have continued with us" (1 John 2:19). God provides a peace that passes understanding, but only to those who spend time with him.

God has also promised us his power. He has promised power to his people. God says, "I'll go with you," and in so doing makes such a difference in our lives. One of the great Bible teachers of our time used this formula: "One plus God equals enough" . . . enough for any occasion! In becoming weak and allowing Him to become our strength, we are made strong. In Christ, but only in him, are all things possible. Without him we can do nothing.

God has promised us that he will be the same in his purpose. He has a job to do, but he can do it only through us. If he has laid his hands on you, if he has led you to do his will, his power will be sufficient for you to do his purpose. We don't "find" time for God; we "take" time for God. Our purpose, in him, is to glorify God and bring others to him.

The Same in His Promises

One songwriter expressed God's promise like this:

He has never broken any promise spoken,
He will keep his promise to me.

God has never broken a promise to us. He has promised that he will save, he will forgive, regardless of the seriousness of the offense, if only we have contrite hearts. We have promised him that we will be faithful, that we will pledge our lives to him. Often when we're in a tight spot we say, "Lord, if you will just answer this prayer, I promise I will . . ." But do we? Do we keep *our* promises?

Jesus has promised to cleanse us from all unrighteousness. What have we promised him?

PRAYER

Our Father, we thank you that, as the Rock of Ages, you do not change. We thank you that you are the same yesterday and today, and that even the atrocious sins of our day you can forgive. Amen.

2   Because He Shed His Own Blood

(Hebrews 9:12, 13:12; Revelation 1:5)

> The church of God, which he hath
> purchased with his own blood
> (Acts 20:28).

I know of no promise as meaningful
to the Christian as the one that Jesus will
cover our sin (cf. Rom. 4:7). There is nothing
we can do with our sins to hide them; they
will not go away. All we can do is ask the
Lord to wash our sins away in the power
of his blood.

Listen to these four Scripture verses,
all of which contain the phrase, "his own
blood."

> Take heed therefore unto yourselves,
> and to all the flock, over the which
> the Holy Ghost hath made you over-
> seers, to feed the church of God,
> which he hath purchased with his
> own blood (Acts 20:28).

Neither by the blood of goats and calves, but by his own blood he entered in once into the holy place, having obtained eternal redemption for us (Hebrews 9:12).

Wherefore Jesus also, that he might sanctify the people with his own blood, suffered without the gate (Heb. 13:12).

Unto him that loved us, and washed us from our sins in his own blood, and hath made us kings and priests unto God and his Father; to him be glory and dominion for ever and ever. Amen (Rev. 1:5-6).

How difficult it is to fathom the depth of the words, "In his own blood . . . with his own blood . . . by his own blood." We as Christians can only stand in awe, recognizing that our reconciliation is made possible through the blood of Jesus Christ.

To speak of Jesus' blood must surely seem repulsive to those who are not Christians. The world can only think of the good life that Jesus lived. We do not like to think of the spilling of Jesus' blood because it is an admission of our sin and guilt. The image of the cross was a stumblingblock to the Greek and to the Jew, and it still remains so for many of us today. Much that is true is distasteful to us because of our carnal appetites. Sin is an unpleasant thought. But it is only when we come to terms with our own sinfulness that we can appreciate the blood of Jesus Christ as the ultimate symbol of love.

A woman who had only a scattered knowledge of Christianity lay on her deathbed. A missionary, with Bible in hand, came to her. The woman asked, "Does your book have anything in it about the blood?" She knew that she was drawing near to the unknown, and she wanted to know more about the protection of God's redemptive blood.

Dwight L. Moody was passing through Utah on a train. The train's engineer was of a different faith. When the engineer learned that Moody was on board, he sent for him to come to the cab. Moody went, and the man began to quote from his own book of scriptures, attempting to convert him. Moody quoted the Bible in response, and the two discussed religion for some time.

As they neared the end of the line, the man had to change shifts with another engineer. Moody got off with him and said, "Sir, let me give you a parting word. After all, there is not so much difference in our religions except this. You serve your religion in terms of 'do's' and we serve ours in terms of 'done.' There isn't anything further we can do to be saved except believe. It's all been done for us on the cross by Christ Jesus."

There is nothing man can bring or buy to save himself, except to cast himself on the grace and mercy of the Lord. The blood of Jesus Christ cleanses us from all sin.

His Own Blood Was Patriarchal!

Jesus the man was a direct descendant of Abraham. He was also of the seed of David. Altogether human in his activity on earth, Jesus was "the Word made flesh." He was entirely human in that he lived in a human body, wearied as we weary, hungered as we hunger, wept as we weep. He suffered in all points as we do, yet he knew no sin. He bled as we do and died just as we do. But he arose by the power of God. That same power enables the Christian to rise also.

His Own Blood Was Perfect!

David cried out, "I was shapen in iniquity; and in sin did my mother conceive me" (Psalm 51:5). What a contrast to the angel's words to Mary concerning the birth of Jesus: "But that holy thing which shall be born of thee shall be called the Son of God" (Luke 1:35)!

Jesus' blood was perfect; it had to be. He took upon himself the form of a man because the sacrifice had to be one man could understand. Jesus' blood was without blemish as a lamb slain before the foundation of the world.

In Old Testament times two goats would be offered on the altar. One goat would be slain and his blood removed by the High Priest into the Holy of Holies and sprinkled on the mercy seat. The other goat was taken into the wilderness, away from the Temple and the people, and left there to die. This goat was the "scapegoat," the one who bore the people's sins away. When John the Baptist came he declared, "Behold the lamb of God, which taketh away the sin of the world" (John 1:29). Jesus became *our* scapegoat.

His Own Blood Was Precious!

Jesus' blood was precious. Precious means "of great value," as in the parable of the pearl of great price. Goats and bulls could no longer take away sin after Jesus came. Only faith in the redemptive blood of Christ would save from sin. Where there is no blood, there is no conviction, no redemption, no salvation.

His Own Blood Is Our Provision!

God's blood is our provision; through him we have life. How? you ask.

First, he is our *substitute*. He took our place on the cross; he suffered there to bear our sins; he bore our burdens. Only he can forgive; only he can blot out sins; only he can sponge the record clean.

Second, he is our *satisfaction*. We have only to look at the cross and we can never doubt God's love.

During my college days we were conducting a revival in a rural community. We asked a man many years our senior to help us, knowing him to be an unusually dedicated man. He later told us that he had been reared in an adjoining community.

During the meeting we visited a home

where an aged mother lived alone. We went into her parlor, and she began to tell us about the pictures of the children hanging on the wall. She said little about one child, and I asked her to tell us more. She skipped over it as quickly as possible.

After our visit, my preacher friend and I went down to the creek bed near the church and walked up and down. He was unusually restless and finally mentioned the boy in the picture.

"You know that boy you asked about? He's in the penitentiary, and I guess I'm as responsible as anyone for his being there. We used to hang around together, and I used to think it was smart to rob the building where I'm preaching now. But God got hold of me and saved me, and that boy is not saved." His shoulders drooped and he began to weep.

"If you knew all those things, why were you willing to come here?" I asked.

"Somebody needs to let these people know that the blood of Jesus can forgive all sin."

Jesus is our provision and our satisfaction.

Remember the story of Simeon in the New Testament? When Mary brought the

baby Jesus to the Temple "to present him
to the Lord," Simeon asked to hold him.
When he had done so he said, "Lord, now
lettest thou thy servant depart in peace, according to thy word; for mine eyes have seen
thy salvation" (Luke 2:29–30). Simeon knew
the satisfaction of having seen Jesus.

We will never experience that in our
lifetime, but we do know satisfaction in re-
alizing that God loves us, and that he loved
us enough to die for us. Had he not loved
us, why would he have died in that way?

Jesus is our Savior. Without the shedding of blood "there is no remission of sin."

What can wash away my sin?
Nothing but the blood of Jesus.
What can make me whole again?
Nothing but the blood of Jesus.

At a conference on the great religions
of the world, representatives of Islam, Hin-
duism, and Christianity spoke at length. By
the time the first two speakers had finished
their eloquent addresses, the Christian had
little time left for his presentation. Addressing the men on the forum, he said, "You
know more about literature than you do the
Bible. Do you remember the scene in *Macbeth* when Lady Macbeth, having partici-

pated in a murder, looks at the bloodstains on her hands and rubs them hysterically, saying, 'Out, out, damn spot'? Do you have anything in your religion that will get rid of the bloodstains?" The Muslim and the Hindu shook their heads. "The only thing that will remove the stain of sin from you and from me," said the Christian, "is the precious and powerful blood of Jesus Christ. He died for our sins!"

Jesus is our Savior as well as our satisfaction.

I once lived in a small town where the primary form of entertainment was to sit outside the Post Office, chatting, whittling, and listening to the talk that went on. One day a group of men sat on the porch steps, discussing all the things God could do. Finally an old black man said, "There's one thing God can't do." The others looked up, shocked. "God can't see my sins after they've been covered with the blood."

That is powerful theology. The blood of Jesus is the only thing that can sponge our sins from our souls and make us whole again. "Though your sins be as scarlet," God said, "they shall be white as snow. Though they be red as crimson, they shall be as wool" (Isa. 1:18).

Thanks be to God for the power of his blood to cleanse us from sin.

PRAYER

Our Father, we are guilty of sin. We recognize that the carnal and the spiritual in us fight daily for the possession of our souls. We are thankful that you have not only forgiven our sins, but blotted them out with the blood of your Son, Jesus Christ. Now create a clean heart and renew a right spirit within us, O God. Amen.

3 Because He Forgives

Forgive, and ye shall be forgiven.
(Luke 6:37).

God never seems more marvelous to us than when we conceive of him as the Forgiver of sin. If there is anything vital to our happiness, our security, our thoughts of eternal life, it is the realization that we need to be forgiven of our sins. But there can be no forgiveness until there is recognition of guilt and confession.

In the name of progress we have made many changes in our life-styles. We have given new labels to old evils. Evils that were once clearly recognized as sin are now welcomed as a way of life.

Hardly any subject should create as much interest as forgiveness, because of our need for it. Yet, the matter of confession is no easy art. I know of no one who has mastered it. Repentance is something we all find hard to come by. None of us likes to admit guilt.

Young people feel that sin is the priority of older people, that it is committed only by those who have accepted responsibility for their own lives. It is easier to blame parents or institutions or government or the authorities than it is to accept responsibility for sin.

Older people, on the other hand, think of sin as an act of aggression. They think, *I don't take an active part against God, therefore I must be for him.* But James said, "To him that knoweth to do good, and doeth it not, to him it is sin" (4:17).

Jesus said that when we pray, we should ask "Forgive us our debts" (Matt. 6:12). Jesus recognized that only as we come before God with an attitude of confession can we accept his forgiveness and in turn forgive others. Confession plus forgiveness equals fellowship.

The illustration of the prodigal son returning home is the clearest portrayal of repentance we have.

Without moral effort there is no confession, and the prodigal paid the price of confession and forgiveness. He came seeking pardon, and when he did he put his heart, soul, and life at his father's disposal and asked to start at the bottom and work his way up.

A genuine confession of sin is a moral readjustment, a turning around. The prodigal son had no intention of carrying on in the same way; he was ready for a change. Mentally as well as morally, he was transformed. He was ready to give up his independence; he was ready to start over. He was simply grateful to be home. When we have readjusted ourselves morally and transformed our mental set, we are emancipated spiritually. The realization that he was forgiven, with the slate wiped clean, freed him and gave him a new start. He was made whole.

Jesus often asked, "Wilt thou be made whole?" (John 5:6). He was speaking, not only of the body, which needed healing, but also of the soul.

The Pharisees accused Jesus of blasphemy when he forgave men of their sins. But Jesus answered, "For whether is easier, to say, Thy sins be forgiven thee; or to say, Arise, and walk? But that ye may know that the Son of man hath power on earth to forgive sins, (then saith he to the sick of the palsy,) Arise, take up thy bed, and go unto thine house" (Matt. 9:5-6). His accusers were trying to pit the physical against the spiritual healing. But Jesus was interested in the whole person. And no person is whole who has not been forgiven. "Confess your faults one to another" was and is sound advice.

Need for Confession

To say that someone is "a good man" is not to say that he is without sin.

Romans 3:23 declares, "All have sinned, and come short of the glory of God." Who would deny that? The Bible speaks sharply against the person who says he knows no sin. John said that the man who saw no sin in his own life was a liar, that the truth was not in him (1 John 1:8,10).

More dangerous than the drunkard is the moralist who does not see the sin in his own life, or his responsibility to his neighbor. A young man asked, "Why can't I burn my house down if I want to? There is no insurance on it; it belongs to me; and it won't hurt anybody." But could the young man be sure that a strong wind wouldn't come along and spread that fire to a neighbor's house?

By the same token, you can't be sure that your behavior won't affect those around you. No man has the right to set a bad example for his neighbor, the children across the street, or the people who live behind him. Every person touches the lives of at least a handful of others. To say, "I'm not doing anything to hurt anybody. Why can't I live the way I want to?" is a refusal to accept responsibility for one's own behavior.

Author A. J. Cronin, in one of his novels, tells of a child who became ill and was taken to the hospital. He was found to have diphtheria, and a tube was inserted in his throat. A nurse was posted to watch by his bedside all night. During the night she fell asleep and awoke to find the child choking. A young woman and new on the job, she lost control and became hysterical. When they had quieted her and the doctor had arrived, the child was dead.

The doctor was furious. He filled out a report on her, noting her error. "Don't you have anything to say? Don't you know that you have just flunked nurse's training?" She stood before him, trembling, and said, "The only thing I have to say is that I want another chance. I want another chance."

Still angry, the doctor told her it was over, sealed his report, and went home to try to sleep. But as he fought for sleep, he began to ask himself the question, "Who am I to play God and to judge?" He recognized the scar that had been left on the life of

the young woman and realized that she
would have to deal with the tragedy all her
life. He tore up the report. "In my old age,"
he said, "it gives me comfort to know that
that young woman is now head of the larg-
est hospital in England."

"Give me another chance" is the cry
of every human soul. We have all needed
another chance at some time, and if it were
not for God's merciful forgiveness and the
tenderness of his love we would not have
been able to wipe the slate clean. "If we confess . . . he is faithful and just to forgive
us our sins . . ." (1 John 1:9).

Kinds of Confession

What kinds of confession are there?
One lesson the Bible teaches us is that the
offense committed should determine the
confession made. Secret sins should be secretly confessed; private sins should be pri-
vately confessed. "For God who heareth in
secret shall forgive you openly."

Likewise, the sin that is done openly
should be confessed openly, at least where
it is openly known.

Now I am not advocating marathon
confessions in groups. Sometimes public
confession can do more harm to the gospel
than it can good to the individual who con-

fesses. Sometimes we find ourselves con-
fessing everyone's sins but our own. It becomes too easy to say, "What's wrong with
the world? People don't love God as they
used to. They don't come to church anymore."

The point of confession is to admit our
own guilt, not to point out what's wrong with
the other individual. When we judge others
we are guilty of the worst kind of sin, the
sin of pride. And Jesus warned us about the
sins of the spirit. Specific confessions,
where we say "I" instead of "you" or "he"
or "they," are more worthy in God's sight.

Personal Confession

Sin is never private or personal; it always reaches out to touch others. "Against
thee and thee only have I sinned, O God,"
confessed David. How could David have
said such a thing? we wonder. He had sinned against his home, the home of another,
the trust of a people, and his army. Yet he
says, "Against thee only have I sinned."
What did he mean?

David's statement points up the difference between an apology and a confession. True, we need to apologize to those we
love when we hurt them, but an apology will
not suffice for God.

Sin is never totally personal. It multiplies until it wrecks countless lives. The only way we can escape its damning curse is to confess it to the Lord, because he is the only one who can change us. And change is the measure of confession. A responsible confession is one in which a person confesses a changed life.

I knew a man in a West Texas community who was as upstanding a man as I have ever known. He attended church regularly but never joined. And the reason he didn't was a reason he couldn't even remember, one that went back thirty years. What a transformation this man could have made in his life and in the lives of others if he had forgiven the people who made him angry once upon a time.

"Judge not that ye be not judged," Jesus says. Do you have a forgiving heart?

PRAYER

Our Father, we recognize that we have been blinded by sin and that we need your forgiveness. We confess our guilt before you today so you may restore us to your service. Amen.

4 Because of His Compassion

(Matthew 9:35-38)

> When he saw the multitudes, he was moved with compassion on them (Matt. 9:36).

Jesus was the most misunderstood man who ever walked the earth. He was judged and prejudged, cursed and crucified. An ancient philosopher once observed that if a perfect man ever walked the earth, he would be killed. Jesus fulfilled that destiny.

Jesus' enemies took a fiendish delight in calling him the "friend of sinners." Yet Jesus himself, had he been in the grave long enough, would probably have chosen that description as an epitaph. All that he did while he was on earth, all that he accomplished in life and in death, was summed up in the phrase, "Friend of sinners." He opened his arms wide to the blind and the lost, the downtrodden and bewildered, the halt and the maimed.

Jesus needs no tombstone, no marker.

Do you realize that there is a difference between a tombstone and a memorial? A tombstone designates where a man has been buried. A memorial says how a man has lived.
Everything good that we observe on this
earth is a true memorial to the concern of
Christ for mankind.

We need no monuments to Jesus—the
two ordinances are memorials enough of
the kind of life he lived.

As often as people are baptized, they
are baptized in the likeness of his death and
raised in the likeness of his resurrection.

As often as people take the fruit of
the vine and the bread, they remember the
shedding of his blood.

As often as we do a good deed in the
name of Jesus Christ, we are patterning our
lives after his.

Jesus had a compassionate heart. His
was and is not insulated against pain and
suffering. He was open to the hurts of this
sin-cursed world.

As one man put it, his was a seismo-
graphic heart. Like the instrument that
measures the movements and rumblings of
the earth, Jesus' heart measured the rumblings of the human soul—the disasters, the
catastrophes, the turmoil. So sensitive was

and is he that he feels all the pain of the world.

What a contrast the life of Jesus is from the holy men of India, who could not touch or be touched by the needs of those around them. How different from those who seclude themselves from the world. Jesus urges us to follow the example of the Good Samaritan, who knelt beside the Jew lying in the dirt, reached under and lifted him up. The others rushed by, on their way to the Temple in Jerusalem or other appointments. They were going to the synagogue to worship; they were paying their debts. They had already given to the Heart Fund, United Givers, the Cancer Drive. Why should they touch a broken man lying beside the road?

In Jesus Christ we have a high priest who is touched by our infirmities. Do we not have an obligation to follow in his footsteps and share our feelings of love and concern for each other?

Concern for Man

Jesus expressed his concern in concrete ways. Verse 35 says that Jesus went all through the cities and villages, "teaching in their synagogues, and preaching the

gospel of the kingdom, and healing every
sickness and every disease among the people." Jesus was busy, and his acts of compassion were more than sympathy, more than
pity. They were an expression of genuine
empathy—his ability to put himself in the
place of others. Isn't that exactly what
Christ did in his ultimate act on the cross?

A familiar expression a few years ago
was, "I can see you, but I can't quite read
you." Doesn't that describe how Jesus may
have felt before he took the form of a man?
He wanted to come in the person of a man
that men might know him better.

Every one of us has a responsibility
to get involved with our fellowmen. We cannot go on indefinitely avoiding contact with
people. We can't hire a staff to do our sing-
ing, our praying, our witnessing, our teaching for us. Sooner or later we must come
face to face with our tasks.

Jesus didn't close his eyes to the de-
formed, the helpless, and the unclean. He
opened his mind, his eyes, his heart. He
wasn't like the man who took the commuter
into New York City each morning, and each
morning, at a certain place along the route,
reached and pulled down the blinds because
he didn't want to look out on the slums.

We cannot pull down the blinds on the injustices of this world forever. The command of Jesus—his example of compassion—speaks too loudly. We may allow ourselves to be annoyed by other people, but if we're busy protecting ourselves, insulating ourselves from pain, we won't let them get close enough to hurt us. Love and caring make us vulnerable. We might get hurt. But isn't that what Christ on the cross is all about?

The Bible gives us several examples of the kind of concern Jesus expects of us. Moses was called to lead his people out of Egypt, and he prayed that he would be blotted out in place of his people.

Abraham repeatedly wept and prayed over his nephew, Lot, in Sodom. Paul wished himself "accursed for his kinsmen's sake."

John Knox, that saint of Scotland, prayed, "Give me Scotland or I die."

Do we know anything about that kind of compassion? Do we do anything about the kind we *do* know?

Compassion for Man

The condition of man was such that Jesus looked out on the multitudes and saw a herd of sheep, unable to rise, their fleece torn and bleeding. What a comparison this is: As Carlyle pointed out, sheep are animals that like to crowd together. They are afraid to be alone; they have no sense of direction. They will follow one another to their own destruction.

How did Christ react when he saw this herd of sheep? He heaved inside with pity. What a graphic description of emotion that is! So distraught was Jesus at the sight that he felt nauseated. How often have we been so moved with concern at the sight of our fellowmen that we felt sick inside?

Several times in the New Testament the word "compassion" is used to describe Jesus' feelings. Let's look at them.

In Matthew 15:32 Jesus looked out over the multitudes and, being "moved with compassion," healed the sick.

In Matthew 20:34 Jesus took compassion on two blind men who were begging for mercy. The crowd rebuked them, telling them to hold their peace, but the rebuke only caused them to cry louder. Jesus heard their plea and returned their sight.

When he healed the centurion's daughter, when he touched the lepers and made them whole, when he released the devil from the man, compassion was the motivating force.

Jesus was concerned, not only for the physical needs of people, but also for the spiritual hunger they felt. He saw them as sheep without a shepherd and felt compassion within.

The Challenge

With such an example before us, how can we meet the challenge?

A young mother, sitting in a hospital waiting room, discovered that her child was dead in her arms. When the doctor learned what had happened, he sent for me, her pastor.

What a difficult thing it was to coax that mother to release the body of her child. How little any of us understood her anguish. And it was not until we found a woman in the hospital who had experienced a similar sorrow that we were able to reach the mother.

Jesus on the cross crying, "My God, my God, why hast thou forsaken me?" is something we can all identify with. Even Jesus, who was and is God's own Son, felt abandoned at his darkest moment. Would we not expect him to understand our own need for compassion and sympathy? Jesus was human and felt our sorrow. He gave us a model to follow. Remember the death of his friend, Lazarus? The Scriptures say simply, "Jesus wept."

What are we to do? We cannot heal as Jesus did. We cannot perform miracles and make the lame walk and the blind see. What can we do where we are?

Jesus said to the disciples, "The harvest truly is plenteous, but the labourers are few; pray ye therefore the Lord of the harvest that he will send forth labourers into his harvest" (Matt. 9:37-38). Pray for the laborers rather than the harvest. Fretting about the harvest won't get the job done; getting the laborers out into the field will make the difference.

Sympathy, even compassion, is not enough if it is not backed by effort. To feel something is only the beginning; to do something about those feelings is the next step. "Rise up, O men of God! Be done with lesser things," goes the hymn.

Have you prayed lately about what you want God to do? Have you prayed about what God wants you to do? If you haven't, begin now.

Pray because the laborers are scarce.

Pray because they have become lazy.

Pray because they have lost their sensitivity to the heartbeat of the world and have trampled the lost.

Pray that we will be revived, stirred in compassion to enter the fields and labor!

Andrew Carnegie was once asked what he would do if he lost his wealth. "You can take away my steel mills, take away my capital, take away all that I have. But leave me my men and we will build the kingdom back again."

Without us as laborers, the fields cannot be harvested. With us as laborers, Christ's compassion and death on the cross will not have been in vain.

PRAYER

O God, we confess that we are insensitive to the problems of those around us. We have grown lazy in our labors of love. We are grateful for your compassion and the love we feel from others. We ask that our own fires of feeling may be rekindled. Amen.

5   Because of His Immortality

(John 8:51; 14:19)

> Whosoever liveth and believeth in
> me shall never die (John 11:26).

Genesis relates that God made man in his own image; that with God's breath of life, "Man became a living soul." If man is made in God's image and God is eternal, do we not automatically inherit the gift of immortality?

In the verse above, Jesus issues an invitation to immortality. Easter and death are paradoxical; physical and spiritual death are not the same. Physical death affects the body, and spiritual death affects the soul *and* the body. "Fear him," said Jesus, "who is able to destroy both soul and body."

When he sinned, Adam died spiritually. He (his body) lived to be 930 years old, but his soul died when he estranged himself from God.

In our day we usually have one of two attitudes toward death: either we think it is everything, or nothing. If we say nothing about it, we think of it as something to experience, to "go through," but as inevitable. Or we see it as everything, a prowler that knows no bounds, a shadow which moves across the face of the earth and has the power to change everything. Madame Curie, on the death of her partner-husband, said, "It is the end of everything . . . everything!" She felt shattered.

It is true that death shatters human plans, defies man's ambition, and is his last enemy. We may dress up the appearance of death, but it is still "death to die." Jesus never conducted funerals—only resurrections. But he never taught a Pollyanna attitude toward death, either. He realized that all of us one day would cease to debate it as an ethical question and would experience it as a personal reality. He realized that man would continue to ask with Job, "If a man die, shall he live again?" (Job 14:14).

The word death is used three different ways in the Bible. In one instance there is a discussion of physical death, the separation of body from spirit. Another mention of death refers to it as cessation, a time when things no longer are. A third mention of death is that of spiritual death, when man is eternally separated from God.

Jesus recognized the power of death and what it could do to the mind of man. More than once he referred to it as a sleep, a rest for the body. When Jesus healed the daughter of Jairus, he told her father that she was sleeping. And when he brought her back to life, the Scriptures say, "The spirit of the daughter returned to her body."

Jesus' acts of healing were also acts of resurrection. He said to the girl, "Arise," and she walked. To one who was sick he said, "Thy faith hath made thee whole." To one crippled from birth, he said, "Go," and the man took up his bed and walked.

But Jesus also emphasized that far worse than separation of spirit from body is separation of man from God. Worse than a mother losing her child? Worse than a loved one lost? Yes. Eternal death is separation, not only from loved ones, but from God as well.

The Bible mentions two resurrections: that of the just and that of the damned. Every soul shall have immortality, but the believer shall enjoy eternal life with God, while the unbeliever must endure *im-mortality away from God.* "He that believeth in me, though he were dead, yet shall he live; he that believeth in me, he shall never die. Believest thou this?" Jesus was asking a most personal question. *Do* we believe?

Immortality

Jesus' mission was twofold and paradoxical: he came to give life, and he came to die. All men come into the world under the sentence of death, but all desire to live forever.

Immortality and eternal life are two different things.

Immortality is the gift of the Creator, an eternal continuous existence of the soul after the death of the body.

Eternal life is the gift of the Savior. Eternal life means it is not death to die. "Because I live, ye shall live also" (John 14:19).

Science admits immortality and describes it as change. The body goes to the grave, yes. It becomes dust, yes. The flesh decays, life changes, the temple of man's body crumbles. But energy is never lost; it is only changed.

The character of God calls for eternal life and describes it as communion. Will death end that communion? If God called us friends, would he cast us off? The character of God demands that there be eternal life.

Religion is communion with God. God walked in the Garden of Eden with man, and man turned his back on God and chose sin. But God so loved man that he could not turn his back on him, and provided Jesus Christ and a cross so that man could return to God.

God hungers for fellowship with man. He enters into friendship with man. Abraham was called a "friend of God." God could not hide his plans from Abraham. God was also a friend of David. Jesus in the New Testament calls his disciples "friends."

If God hungers for fellowship with man, if Jesus gathered a close circle of friends about him, if God cared enough to send his Son to die, would he then allow the coffin to become the conqueror? Wouldn't it be strange for him to annihilate us, to remove us from his presence forever? It is not in God's character to do so. He is God of the living, not of the dead.

Intellect

If we have been made in God's image,
that image also includes an intellect. "Let
this mind be in you which was also in Christ
Jesus" wrote Paul (Phil. 2:5). Our intellect
teaches us that some day the wrongs of the
world will be righted. Someday there will
be justice for those who have been treated
unjustly or who have treated others unjustly. Pilate sat on his throne while Christ
hung on a cross. The rich man burning in
hell had all the good things in life while
Lazarus, now in heaven, had suffered
greatly on earth. Wrongs will be righted and
ignorance wiped away. Partial knowledge
will give way to full understanding.

Why did God create us in his image,
with a portion of his intellect? Because he
wanted us to see and know. And he gave
us Jesus Christ to reveal to us the immortality that men through all times have searched
and groped for.

Jesus came back to let people know
that he had risen. He was seen of Cephas,
of the twelve, of 500, of James, of the apostles, and also, wrote Paul, of Paul. "Now if
Christ be preached that he rose from the
dead, how say some among you that there

is no resurrection of the dead? But if there
be no resurrection of the dead, then is Christ
not risen: . . . For as in Adam all die, even
so in Christ shall all be made alive" (1 Cor.
15:12-13, 22).

If Jesus has not been resurrected and
we have been preaching in vain, Paul said,
then is no man resurrected, and we are "of
all men most miserable."

But what about our resurrection? you
ask. Will we know each other in heaven?
Dwight Moody had a good answer for that
question. "Don't you think we will have
more sense in the perfect body than we have
here now in the imperfect body? If we recognize each other now, don't you think we will
recognize each other then?"

Paul tells us, "It is sown a natural
body; it is raised a spiritual body" (15:44).
The mortal body must put on immortality
before death can be swallowed up in victory.
"To be absent from the body," wrote Paul,
"is to be present with the Lord."

Immediacy

"In a moment, in the twinkling of an
eye, at the last trump: for the trumpet shall
sound, and the dead shall be raised incorruptible, and we shall be changed," writes

Paul of the resurrection of man (15:52). The resurrection will be immediate. Immediately death's victory will be swallowed up as we enter the presence of God.

"Life is like the day and death is like the sunset," someone has mused. If that is so, then heaven is the happiest morning, the first day of forever. Paul teaches us that there is no soul-sleep, that there is not death, that we move out of this body and directly into the presence of God. Didn't Jesus promise the thief on the cross, "To day, shalt thou be with me in paradise"?

After his death Jesus appeared on land, on the sea, and in the air. That his tomb was found empty is a promise that all believers will one day be resurrected.

We have much to look forward to! Nearly twenty years ago I attended a meeting in Nashville. J. B. Lambdin, who was head of the Training Union Department for some forty years, had just retired. He had written his last report and was to be honored at a dinner on a Tuesday evening. But he passed away Sunday and was buried on Tuesday.

When we came back to consider his report, which had been written a week before his death, we read these closing words:

"The best is yet to be!" The sting of death was gone, and for J. B. Lambdin, as for all of us, the best was yet to be.

Thanks be to God who gives us the victory over death through our Lord Jesus Christ.

PRAYER

God our Redeemer, we confess that we tremble in the face of the unknown and accept thy assurance that Jesus Christ paid our debt on the cross. We rejoice in his resurrection and in his victory over death. Amen.

6 Because of Answered Prayer

(James 5:16; Romans 8:26-27)

> The effectual fervent prayer of a
> righteous man availeth much
> (James 5:16).

We talk more about prayer and know
less about it than any subject in the Bible.
Sometimes we feel we pray and there is no
answer. The skeptic says, Why bother trying
to change God's mind anyway? But a Christian has achieved some maturity when he
recognizes that he does not have to understand everything and accepts some things
on faith.

Sometimes we are protected by unanswered prayer. Look at three cases of unanswered prayer in the Bible.

Remember the Gadarene demoniac?
Filled with an evil spirit over which he had
no control, the man was miserable. His case
seemed hopeless. There was no reason for
him to live, yet God came through to heal
him.

When Jesus laid his hand on him, the
man in gratitude cried out, "Lord, can I go
with you?" Strange, isn't it, that Jesus' response to this man who would have done
anything to serve him was, "No, you stay
here." Was Jesus insensitive to the man's
gratitude? Was he unsympathetic to his desire to repay the debt? No, he knew that the
man's greatest need was to glorify God, and
that he could best do that where he was
known.

Don't we sometimes believe that, if
we were in another place, we could be serv-
ing God more fully? Often the best chance
we have of glorifying God is right in the
spot where we raised the question.

Then there was the example of Paul
who prayed, "Lord, remove this thorn from
my flesh." We do not know, though many
guesses have been made, what Paul's thorn
was. But we are certain of one thing—he
wanted to be rid of it. Whatever it was, it
may have been the one factor that kept Paul
close to Christ.

It appears that Paul's prayer was
never answered, yet Paul talks more about
answered prayer, and in more glowing
terms, than any of the other apostles. Paul
seemed to understand that God knew what

was best for him, and he tried to remain submissive to the will of God.

One of the most striking prayers in the Bible is the prayer of Jesus in the garden of Gethsemane. Imagine the Master, head drooping, his heart already broken and the blood flowing freely. In his pathos and genuine agony he cries out, "Father, if it be possible, let this cup pass from me!" It must have seemed to him that the heavens were dark, the doors were shut, and no answer came.

Yet think on this for a minute. Suppose God had answered that prayer. Suppose somehow Jesus had miraculously been removed from that cross and spared that cruel death. Where would we be today? We would have had no message of immortality, no resurrection on Easter, no redemption from sin, no eternal life.

Job struggled with the question of unanswered prayer, because if ever a man did not hear his prayers answered, it was Job. Job with his boils, his plagues, his family's trials, his crop losses. We can scarcely blame him for asking, "What profit should we have if we pray unto him?" Yet Job's faith was steady to the end.

Today some of us are asking Job's question. Where will it get me if I pray? It doesn't really help. Or we might ask, Why pray, anyway? If God knows everything, why do we need to pray? Doesn't he know what we need?

Some feel that prayer is mere auto-suggestion, that we suggest things to ourselves in prayer and then set about to do them, giving the credit to God. Still others want to know what we hope to accomplish by prayer. Are we trying to change God's mind? Give him advice?

What prayer does is change, not only things, but also the one who prays. And isn't that often exactly what's needed? Not to get God to do something for us, but to change us to be submissive to his will?

I once prayed so intensely, with such a heavy burden on my heart, that I felt sure there must come an answer. Yet I knew all the while that there was no answer, that the door was shut on my request. But the door was not shut completely, because the praying made me submissive to God's will. Prayer changes the one who prays. But it also changes circumstances.

Andrew Carnegie once was discussing the matter of God, prayer, and power with a friend. Carnegie asked his friend, "Now, why should I pray? Tell me, why do I need it? Name one thing that God could give me that I don't already have." His friend replied, "He might give you humility."

Some years ago a New England fisherman went to sea with his sails out. A storm arose off the coast, and the crew realized that they were in danger. The men gathered on deck and looked at the captain. "Will we ever get back?" they wanted to know.

The old captain took from his pocket a large gold watch. "About this time every evening my wife is praying for my safe return," he said, looking at the face of the watch. "Now, I am not a God-fearing person like my wife, but let's put our shoulders to the wheel, take down the sails, and help God answer her prayer."

Prayer is more caught than taught, and that old sea captain had caught the spirit of prayer from his wife. The message was: Do and believe at the same time.

We have responsibility in prayer. God does not expect us to sit back and wait for him to do all the work; he expects for us to work by his side. Dwight Moody, at the height of his evangelistic career, was traveling down the Mississippi on a river boat. The boat caught on fire, and Moody joined the bucket brigade.

One man, frightened and nearly hysterical, said to Moody, "Don't waste your time carrying water; get down on your knees and pray." Moody replied, "I can pray a lot more enthusiastically if I carry the water and pray at the same time."

Prayer is not a substitute for laziness. Prayer is living communion, a relationship between ourselves and One who means everything.

Isn't it conclusive enough for us that Jesus prayed? The disciples knew that God was the source and the answer to prayer, and asked to be taught. From Jesus they caught the spirit, the intent, and the point of prayer.

Where Shall We Pray?

Do you like to be with those you love? Of course, you do. Isn't it strange then that you and I, who call ourselves children of God, don't spend any more time in his presence than we do?

"Well, where can I find the time and place to do that?" you ask. "The house is so noisy with the kids and the TV. There isn't time to drive to the church every time you want to talk something over with God."

True. But there should be some solitary place you can go without much trouble.

Jesus sought solitary places. The garden, the mountain, the desert, the boat, the seashore. A parking lot may be one of the few solitary places left. A cemetery in a small town. Home, if there is no one there, or your backyard. The office, if you can close your door for a few moments. Wherever you can be alone with yourself for a few moments is a good place for prayer. If we neglect it, our spirits will dry up and die.

"Well, we have family altar," you answer. Or, "We pray at the dinner table." Yes, and that is fine. But we all say things to God that we would not even say to another living being, not even to a member of our family, because we know that no one loves us as God does.

It is also important to pray with others. When we gather together, Jesus said, our prayers will be answered. This is not the prayer of the publican or the hypocrites that Jesus spoke of. He was not talking of gathering a crowd together as if for a pep rally, brass band and all. He was not speaking of voices lifted high in beautiful words.

Jesus was calling for prayers of confession, submission, and intercession. He was suggesting that, when we gather together, we ought to pray for something or someone of interest and concern to all those gathered. When a fellow Christian leads us in prayer, he is simply voicing the petition each of us feels in our hearts, and we are saying "Amen."

If you want to know a man, pray with him. A man reveals himself quicker in his prayer life than he does anywhere else.

Pray both in solitude and in public. Pray with others.

Pray anywhere and everywhere.

When Shall We Pray?

Jesus arose a great while before day, according to the Scriptures. He selected the early-morning hours on some occasions; on others he simply prayed when he felt the need. But did Jesus wait for a great need to arise?

He prayed before he ministered to people.

He prayed when he set about choosing disciples.

He prayed in the midst of crises and whenever he felt the need.

He defined his position clearly: "Men ought always to pray, and not to faint" (Luke 18:1).

Prayer is not so much "getting God"

to do something as it is "letting God" do something. Prayer is not so much "changing the mind of God" as it is "changing the mind of man" so that man will fit harmoniously into God's pattern.

What Should We Pray?

Isn't it a pity when children grow up and no longer have need of their parents? The moment is so special when a child bursts in without ceremony and asks you for something that means the world to him and you are able to give it. "If you know how to give good gifts to your children, how much more does your heavenly Father know how to give good gifts to them that ask him?" (Author's translation of Matt. 7:11). Do you feel that you treat your child better than your heavenly Father treats you?

Jesus told us how to pray by giving us a model prayer. This was not his prayer for himself, but an example for us to follow. "After this manner pray ye," instructed Jesus.

His prayer included worship. We honor God's name.

It included a personal request. We ask for daily bread.

It mentioned others. We ask forgiveness when we violate others' rights.

Our children, when they were quite small, were saying their prayers one evening. The youngest prayed first. She prayed for her family, each member by name, and then for others she loved—and for those around the world. The older boy had grown weary of listening to her prayer, and kept his own short. As soon as he finished, the little one said, "You didn't pray for me!" We need to pray for each other.

We pray because prayer changes us. In Luke 9:29 we read that, as Jesus prayed on the Mount of Transfiguration, "The fashion of his countenance was altered, and his raiment was white and glistering." He talked with Moses and Elias (Elijah), who spoke to him concerning his death. As Jesus prayed, he was filled with the Holy Spirit, and he admonished his disciples to wait and pray until they were "endued with power"— until there was a change in them.

In 1824 John Quincy Adams and Andrew Jackson were candidates for the presidency. Popular vote brought them to an exact tie, and the matter of settling the tie was left to the House of Representatives. Again the race was very close, and the members of the House rushed to those who had not yet voted.

One man, being urged to vote for Adams, replied, "But I do not personally like him."

"This is not a question of personality but of principle," replied the politician. "You dare not cast such a decisive vote until you have made it a matter of prayer."

Two men were approached this way, and the vote was decided. Prayer made the difference, and Adams was elected.

Luther said, "The less I pray, the harder it gets . . . The more I pray the better it goes."

Jesus prayed all the way through the New Testament.

He prayed at his baptism.

He prayed about his popularity.

He prayed over human madness.

He prayed at the Transfiguration.

He prayed for Peter.

He prayed in the garden of Gethsemane.

He prayed on the cross.

With that kind of example, can we do anything but pray?

PRAYER

Our heavenly Father, teach us to pray. Teach us there are no unanswered prayers. Teach us to be submissive to thy wonderful spirit. Teach us that prayer is communion with Christ. Change us to be submissive to thy will, through prayer. Amen.

7 Because of His Claims

(John 5:18,10:30,42; Matthew 26:63-65)

> Jesus said unto them, . . . before
> Abraham was, I am (John 8:58).

Many statues of Jesus stood along the most prominent road of entry into an old city of Austria. The statues represented various phases of Jesus' ministry. One statue portrayed him as a carpenter, another as a shepherd, another as a physician, another as a sower of seed.

As people would come to the city for business or shopping, they would stand before one statue or another, gazing at the one with which they most closely identified. Those who were craftsmen would stand before the statue of the carpenter. Those who were farmers would gaze up at the sower. Those who were sick would concentrate on Jesus the physician, and so on.

Each of us sees Jesus as we need to see him. I remember the minister who used to tell his congregation not to refer to God as Father, since not everyone's father was good and the word might have a negative connotation. Still, we tend to think of God as a loving father encircling us in his arms and protecting us from harm.

Jesus asked his friends on occasion who they thought he was. "Whom do men say that I the Son of man am? And they said, Some say that thou art John the Baptist; some, Elias; and others, Jeremias, or one of the prophets. He saith unto them, But whom say ye that I am? And Simon Peter answered and said, Thou art the Christ, the Son of the living God" (Matt. 16:13-16). Simon had been with Jesus a long while, and he no longer wondered.

Whom did Christ himself say that he was? What claims did he make for himself?

Jesus Christ made more unusual claims for himself than anyone who has ever walked the earth. He made more incredible claims than Muhammad, Buddha, or any of the other leaders of great world religions. Jesus Christ claimed to be the Son of God.

In John 10:30 Jesus says, "I and my Father are one."

In John 8:42 he says, "I proceedeth

forth and came from God; neither came I of myself, but he sent me."

Jesus gave us no neutral ground. People often alibi, "Well, I can accept that Jesus is a good man, a moral teacher, but I cannot accept that he was the Son of God." How can one say that a man who claims to be God is a good man if he is not God? When Jesus says, "All power is given to me in heaven and earth," either he is telling the truth or he is a madman. We either have to believe him or find his claims silly, impossible, and write him off completely. How could we accept as a moral teacher a man we couldn't trust? How could we say, "I wouldn't like him for a Savior, but I will accept him as a moral teacher"? If we can't believe him when he claims to be God, why should we believe anything else he says?

Listen to Jesus' claims.

"I, if I be lifted up, will draw all men unto me."

"I am the Lord of the sabbath."

"I can destroy the Temple."

"I have power over all mankind."

"I and the Father are one."

"The world shall pass away, but not one jot or tittle of my words shall pass away."

His positive, assertive claims drove the Jews to fury, exasperated them, filled them with hatred. As one author wrote, "He is the supreme egotist of all life." But what did Thomas say? "My Lord and my God."

"Never a man spake like this man spake," said some. "Even the winds and the waves obey his will," said others.

The best way to discover what Jesus thought of himself is to study the titles he used in speaking of himself. Consider these: Messiah, Son of God, Son of man.

Greatest Human Event

The incarnation was the greatest human event in history. True, it went unnoticed by the majority in Bethlehem. The eyes of men are focused on themselves and seldom see beyond. So many mighty men have gone unnoticed until after their deaths. Asked what was new the morning Lincoln was born, a rural mail carrier replied, "Nothing much." When it comes to greatness, we are truly shortsighted.

John 1:14 records the message, "The Word was made flesh." Here was a heaven-sent revelation telling us that God had become man. The prophecies of the Old Testament had become realities. God was now

Emmanuel: God-with-us.

God's claim for Jesus was that he was born of a virgin and conceived of the Holy Spirit. This made Jesus the *God-man*—as much God as though he were never man, as much man as though he were never God. God-with-us was equal to God, the second person in the Trinity.

At the same time Jesus was God-with-us, he was also Son of man. "He took not upon him the form of angels but he took on him the seed of Abraham." Elsewhere the Bible says he was "made of a woman" and "made like unto his brethren."

Yet it is clear that Jesus was set apart. Though one of us, he was never like us, never at home on earth. He who had heaven for home, who was "with" and "before Abraham," was homeless on earth, both at birth and in the grave. "The Son of man hath no place to lay his head," states Matthew 8:20. But was it only his head he could not put to rest? Or was it also his heart? The words of the song tell us "I can't feel at home in this world anymore."

I was speaking on Jesus' humanity once many years ago and a man stood to inquire, "Do you mean to say that Jesus was a man as lonely as I am, as hungry as I have

been, as tempted as I have been?" Yes, indeed! Jesus was tempted, he thirsted, he
hungered, he suffered as few men have suffered, yet he was without sin.

Standing before the Jews, Jesus de-
manded, "Which of you convinceth me of
sin?" (John 8:46) They could only search for
some other accusation, such as, "Say we not
well that thou art a Samaritan, and hast a
devil?" (8:48) Jesus was not *a* Son of man—
he was *the* Son of man.

Greatest Divine Event

Several places in the Scriptures we
are told that the heavenly Father spoke out
concerning the divinity of Jesus! In Matthew 3:17 we hear a voice from heaven at
his baptism, saying, "This is my beloved
Son, in whom I am well pleased." We hear
the same words on the Mount of Transfiguration, with Peter and James and John as
witnesses.

Jesus chastises unbelievers in John 5,
saying, "And the Father himself which hath
sent me, hath borne witness of me. Ye have
neither heard his voice at any time, nor seen
his shape. And ye have not his word abiding
in you: for whom he hath sent, him ye believe not. Search the scriptures: for in them

ye think ye have eternal life: and they are they which testify of me." Check out the Word of God, Jesus says; you will find me in its pages.

Why had no one listened to Simeon? Simeon knew he had seen the Christ child.

A "greater than Solomon is here," says Luke 11:31 of Jesus. And Jesus was one who existed "before Abraham," according to John 8. The Word made flesh! The Word of God!

Jesus is the holy one of promise spoken of in Genesis. He is the one prophesied of men. He is the precious one of whom Simeon said, "Mine eyes have seen my salvation."

Greatest Redeeming Event

John had told us that the Word was made flesh.

Paul tells us that Jesus "was made sin" for our sakes. Jesus came to redeem. That was his sole, his whole purpose for being on earth.

Furthermore, he died on the cross like a man, like a man made of flesh; but he rose from the grave like the Son of God he claimed to be. "He was made alive," Luke writes. "He showed himself alive after his

passion" (Acts 1:3). And in 1 Corinthians
15:25 we learn that he is now reigning in
his mediatorial kingdom. "For the Son of
man is come to seek and to save that which
was lost" (Luke 19:10).

Jesus was his earthly name; Christ
was his Messianic (saving) name; "King of
Kings" is his reigning name. "Today thou
shalt be with me in paradise," he promised
the thief on the cross.

Other men have said they would live
after death. Let us ask those who went
before to speak from the tombs of yesterday.

Plato, where are you? Socrates, where
are you? Confucius, where are you? All three
would have to answer from the grave.

But Jesus, Jesus of Nazareth, where
are you? The answer resounds from heaven!

In Old Testament times there was a
section of the Temple known as the Holy
of Holies. Only the High Priest could enter.
He would appear in his robe, bells tinkling
on his vesture, and he would take the people's offering into the inner sanctuary, praying that the gift would be acceptable to God.
A rope was always tied about his feet so if
he died inside the holy space, he would be
pulled out, for that was the dwelling place
of God. If they could hear the bells, they

could assume the priest was still alive.

Jesus, the Bible tells us, went into the Holy of Holies once and for all, and the veil of the Temple was rent. Once and for all a priest was not needed to intercede before God; Jesus had become the High Priest, interceding for us in heaven.

Through his life, his death on the cross, and his resurrection from the grave, "God hath highly exalted him and given him a name which is above every name" (Phil. 2:9).

Jesus is the Son of God, born of a virgin, conceived of the Holy Spirit. He is the bright and morning star, the lily of the valley, the rose of Sharon. He came to seek and to save a lost mankind, and that means you and me. How can we refuse?

PRAYER

Poor indeed, our Father, are the words we have to express your indescribable love. But we confess our belief in the God-man, God-with-us, Jesus Christ. We believe that the birth, death, and resurrection of Jesus are the greatest redeeming events in the history of the world. And we say thank you. Amen.

8   Because of His Church

(Matthew 16:13-18; Ephesians 5:23-24; Acts
2:42-47; 5:41-42)

> Upon this rock I will build my
> church (Matthew 16:18).

Many feel that this century will write
a telling epitaph for the church. Not only
is God dead, they say, but the church marks
the grave as a tombstone.

Jesus said, "Upon this rock I will build
my church; and the gates of hell shall not
prevail against it" (Matt. 16:18). This is not
only a promise but an assertion! If the
church of God is protected by its Author
against the gates of hell, surely it is insulated against contemporary critics.

Not that the critics don't bear listening to; the church must be more than an
armory and an anchor.

If it is not relevant, then it will be ri-
diculous.

If it is not contemporary, then it will
be condemned.

If it is not meaningful, then it will be meaningless.

Perhaps we the church need to look to the Bethel of Jerusalem for direction. Perhaps the church needs to cast off its burial clothes of trivia and seek a resurrection of its early-day power.

When the world cries out that the church is meaningless, the Word assures us that it is meaningful. As C. S. Lewis said, "God forgive us for listening to the squeak of the usher's shoes when there is majestic music to hear and undimmed glory to be seen!"

Meaning

What is the meaning of the church?

A group of men were discussing the church while standing about at a civic club. As they were talking a minister walked by, and the man leading the discussion reached over and pulled the preacher into the circle. "See," he said, "he'll agree with me. Let's just ask him." To the minister he said, "Tell me, don't you agree that you can get to heaven without belonging to the church?"

The minister stood there for a minute before he replied, then said, "Yes, I believe that it is possible for a man to get to heaven without belonging to the church."

"See?" the man said to the group, "what did I tell you?"

They started to walk away, but the preacher stopped them and said, "Now I want to ask you a question. You asked me if you could get to heaven without going to church. I'm wondering why, if you care nothing for the church, where they sing the songs of Zion, talk about the things of God, are saved by the Lord and praise him, you would want to go to heaven in the first place?"

The Greek word for church is *ekklesia,* which literally means "the called out ones." Even before the time of Christ and the establishment of the church as we know it, many were "called out by God." God called Abraham, saying, "Get thee up and get thee out of this land unto the land that I will show you."

He called Noah, saying, "Noah, call out the people of God," and Noah called the people to repentance and into the ark.

He called Lot, saying, "Lot, get your family and call them out of this place of Sodom and Gomorrah."

As a spiritual body, we are called out by God, called out from all sections of the city and the world, called to gather together as a "church" to worship and glorify God.

We are following the tradition of the New
Testament, where the church is defined as
a local body of baptized believers.

Yet God's church, his kingdom, is not
synonymous with denomination. Christ
made the church; man made the denomination. The church is a monumental thought
in the mind of man and in the heart of God.
It is a colony of heaven on earth, the realm
of the redeemed. We do not go to the cata-
combs or to the cathedral because of the
place, but because of the majestic person
of Jesus Christ who draws us there.

One of the symbols of the church's
foundations that Jesus used was that of the
rock: "Upon this rock I will build my
church." And the psalmist in 18:31 asks,
"Who is a rock save our God?"

Paul refers to the church as a building, "one body in Christ" He didn't use that
word as we do. We speak of meeting at the
"church," meaning the church building.
Paul meant a unified structure as the body
is a structure. "For as we have many members in one body, and all members have not
the same office: So we, being many, are one
body in Christ, and every one members one
of another" (Rom. 12:4-5).

Does one arm delight at the loss of
the other? No! The nervous system is so put

together that, when one part of the body hurts, other parts hurt as well. Jesus said the body of Christ is the same. "When one part of the body of Christ suffers, we all suffer."

Elsewhere in the Bible the church is referred to as the "bride of Christ." When Paul refers to the church as the bride, he mentions Christ as the bridegroom. When a bridegroom loves the bride, you can't criticize the bride and expect the bridegroom to bless you. Just so, you can't take a critical attitude toward the church and expect God to pat you on the head and thank you.

One year on Valentine's Day some children called on me in the study and left me some mementos of the season. Each of them had made a picture of a Valentine with the words, "May the Lord bless you." All except one, that is, whose Valentine read, *"Let* the Lord bless you."

What special insight that child had! Surely the Lord will bless us, as individuals and as his church, if only we let him.

Membership

A regenerated membership of baptized believers is the only basis for membership in a New Testament church. The church is not a gallery of saints talking to

themselves in pious tones of Pharisaism.
The church is a training school of believing
recruits who wish to grow in grace.

A young boy descending into the
water to be baptized expressed disappoint-
ment that none of his kinfolk was there.
"Everyone here," the preacher reassured
him, "is your brother and sister in Christ."

Jesus told us that he was going away,
but he assured us that he would send his Holy
Spirit to comfort us. "And greater works
than I have done ye will be able to do."

The disciples had trouble understanding this; they had seen his miracles, his following, his power. While he was here, he
was working with them. After he went
away, he worked through the disciples, just
as he is now working *through* us.

"You wait and tarry," he said to the
church, "and I shall empower you." He
doesn't minister through an organization.
He doesn't bless methods. He doesn't dedi-
cate a pew. He doesn't make the "laws" of
Sunday School growth divine. He blesses
and empowers *people* like you and me and
gives us a message to proclaim. Through
us and through the power of the Holy Spirit,
Jesus ministers to a lost and dying world.

The gravest danger to the church is
thinking that our assets are what we see

in stone—in the building—rather than in the Spirit. What we have to give, through the Spirit of God, is something money cannot buy. All God asks is what Peter offered, "Silver and gold have I none, but such as I have give I thee." The world can get almost anything it wants today—medicine from Medicare, goods from the government. The only thing it can't get is the Bread of life; that it must get from the believer, with the power of Christ.

Message

A popular minister kept a sign on his pulpit that said, "Do you have a message that will help my people today?"

What is the message of Christ? The message is love: "For God so loved the world that he gave his only begotten Son."

A message for trouble: "I will never leave you nor forsake you."

A message about temptation: "Resist the devil and he shall flee from you."

A message concerning life: "What shall it profit a man if he gain the world and lose his own soul?"

A message to sinners: "If we confess our sins, he is faithful and just to forgive us our sins, and to cleanse us from all unrighteousness."

A message about death: "He that believeth in me shall never die; believest thou
this?"

A sure word about death: "O death,
where is thy sting?"

A sure word about salvation: "Believe
on the Lord Jesus Christ, and thou shalt be
saved."

We have a message—a message of
hope and life, a message of salvation. And
who is preaching this message but you and
me and the other children of God? Let us
rise up to our highest and noblest selves and
let the Spirit of God bless the world through
us, the people, the church. For the church
is the only saving love left in this world.

PRAYER

Our Father, we thank thee for the
church, where we have been loved, visited,
taught, prayed for, and won to the "lamb
of God." O Spirit of love, hover over your
people, the church. Make us a colony of
heaven that we may be the kind of light
to shine in any darkness so that people may
find the way, not to the church, but to you.
Amen.

9 Because of His Promised Return

(Matthew 24:36-46; Luke 21:27-28; 1 Thessalonians 4:13-18)

> I will come again and receive you unto myself (John 14:3).

The word "advent" means coming. The first time Jesus came to earth he came in humiliation. When he comes again, it will be in glory, and "every tongue should confess that Jesus Christ is Lord." There is no more sublime theme in the Scriptures than that of Jesus' return.

During the 1840s the Irish were suffering a potato famine and jobs were scarce. In order to help provide work, the government began a road-building project. One of the workmen was heard to say, "I wouldn't mind being a part of something that had a purpose. But we are building roads that lead to nowhere."

Sometimes we become so busy with "busy work" that we forget what our purpose was and do not realize any longer why we are doing what we do.

The same thing happened in Old Testament times. Men decided to build a tower to heaven for their own glory. But God confounded their languages and made it impossible for them to understand each other, and they had to abandon their stones and mortar. Theirs was a road to nowhere.

We today give our energy to our businesses, our vocations, our pleasures, but after a while we see them go up in smoke. With feelings of futility and depression, we realize we have built roads to nowhere. What we forget is that men who build empires eventually lie in graves covered with weeds, unless they take into account the second coming of Christ. We might as well build castles in the sand, for they are no sooner finished than the tide has come and washed them away.

That which we do for the Lord is permanent. It is present; it is ongoing; it is eternal. We are not building roads to nowhere; we are building on the solid rock of Christ.

That which we do for vanity or pride or material gain is temporary. As James, the younger brother of Jesus, said, "What is your life? It is even a vapour, that appeareth for a little time, and then vanisheth away" (4:14).

Ask the farmer. He tills the soil, plants the seed, waters and nurtures his crop, only to see a whirlwind, storm, or drought leave nothing in its path but a scorched earth.

Ask the child, who builds towers with his wooden blocks, and in a fit of anger kicks them down.

All of our projects are futile unless there is a supreme objective to our lives, a goal governing our actions, something in which we firmly believe.

A Sunday School teacher said to a member of her class, "Do you believe the grapes in the Promised Land were so large that it took two men to carry a cluster of them?"

"That's what the Bible says," the lady replied.

The teacher pressed her. "Do you believe it?"

Again the lady dismissed the question. "It's in the Bible."

In a more personal manner the teacher pressed again. "But do *you* believe it?"

What matters is what you and I believe. Believing in the return of Jesus is what William Barclay describes as believing in one of the "eccentricities of our faith." Yet when the judgment of God has

come and the earth as we know it is finished,
the King of heaven will ask if we believe,
and an answer such as "It's in the Bible"
will not suffice.

To believe in the second coming offers
us a great deal of comfort. An old saint said
to a group of young ministers, "Brethren,
if I had my life to live over, I would spend
more time preaching messages of comfort
to my people. The clearest message of comfort I know is that one day righteousness
will triumph, and good will reign over evil."

"Eschatology" is a word meaning
"doctrine of the last things." There are three
views of the "millennium," which literally
means "one thousand years." The "post-mil-
lenial" view is that Jesus will come after
the world has gotten much better. But history repeats itself, over and over; and while
we may be improving technologically, there
is little evidence—judging from the number
and type of wars in this century alone—that
we are really improving.

The "amillennial view" is that there
is no millennium at all—that the one thousand years is not to be taken seriously. In
2 Peter 3:8 we read, "But beloved, be not ig-
norant of this one thing, that one day is with
the Lord as a thousand years, and a thou-

sand years as one day." Amillennialists quote this verse to show that time in God's mind is not measured by clocks or calendars.

I suppose that I am a "premillennialist." I believe that God, at some hour of his choosing, will return to set this world free. But I feel like the minister who was being interviewed by a pulpit committee. They asked, "What is your position on the second coming of Jesus?"

"I'm for it!" he responded

When they pressed him further, he said deliberately, "I'll tell you. I'm on the program committee, not the time and place committee. I'm just trying to get myself and the people ready, and I'm not worrying about the hour or the day."

Promise of His Coming (John 14:3)

That Jesus is coming is certain. That promise is clearly stated 318 times in the New Testament! And, as G. Campbell Morgan used to say concerning the promises of God, "We have the word of a gentleman on it."

Because there are some things we *don't know* doesn't mean there are some things we *cannot know.* The people who

lived around Noah should have known that
something was about to happen, but they
didn't. Matthew 24:37-39 says,

> But as the days of Noe were, so shall
> also the coming of the Son of man
> be. For as in the days that were before
> the flood they were eating and drink-
> ing, marrying and giving in mar-
> riage, until the day that Noe entered
> into the ark, and knew not until the
> flood came, and took them all away;
> so shall also the coming of the Son
> of man be.

Person of His Coming (Acts 1:11)

The Scriptures tell us that *Jesus himself,* accompanied by his holy angels, will
be coming. He will not send a deputy in his
place.

Some have theorized that the presence of the Holy Spirit is Jesus' second coming. Some have thought that our death will
be the second coming. Some have said that
conversion is his second coming, when he
enters the heart of man.

But the Scriptures make it plain that
the Lord himself—visibly, bodily, literally,
actually, and personally—will return! "This

same Jesus, which is taken up from you into heaven, shall so come in like manner as ye have seen him go into heaven."

Program of His Coming (1 Thess. 4:13-18)

We have three descriptions in the New Testament of Jesus' second coming. According to the book of Revelation, he will come "as a thief in the night." In Matthew he is described as a bridegroom coming for his bride, secretly and softly.

We find a third description in 1 Thessalonians 4, where the Lord takes the world by storm, descending "from heaven with a shout, with the voice of the archangel, and with the trump of God." He stands as though in the midst of lightning, before an adoring universe, so that every eye shall see him coming in glory!

Purpose of His Coming (Titus 2:13)

According to the Scriptures, there will be two resurrections, one for the just and one for the unjust, and the two will be at different times. The saved will enjoy a reunion, where they will be joined with their loved ones forever.

"I do not know what the world is coming to," said one church member to another.

"Nor I," replied his friend, "but I do know who is coming to the world."

In one thirteen-month period I lost the three dearest friends I had in the ministry. I was comforted by the words of F. B. Meyer to his friend, G. Campbell Morgan: "We have never had much time to be together. It looks as though I'm going home before I get to see you. It will please me if God will put our cottages close in heaven so that we can visit there as much as we like."

The early Christians greeted each other with "Our Lord cometh" or "Come, Lord." The promise gave them hope.

A man who owned a large department store had lost a son in World War I and had never recovered from it. For him, Veterans Day, November 11, was very real. One November 11, not long after the war's end, in the middle of the day when the store was full of people, the owner had a Boy Scout stand on the balcony and play taps. The cash registers grew silent, the people stopped talking, and a hush fell over the store as the notes were played.

As the Scout finished, one woman rushed out of the store, forgetting her change. The clerk caught her and put it in her hand. She looked down and said, "What's money now?"

One of these days when the end of time has come and Jesus has returned to reclaim his own, you may ask, "But what about my business, my golf, my vacation, my country club, my family?" And he will answer, "They don't matter now."

PRAYER

Our Father, we look to you to guide our lives today, so that when you come again, we will be ready. Amen.

10 Because of His Indwelling Spirit

(Romans 8:1-16; Acts 1:1-8; John 14:15-18, 16:5-11)

> He shall give you another comforter, that he may abide with you forever (John 14:16).

Now, perhaps more than ever, there is a great deal of interest in the Holy Spirit. Sometimes the Holy Spirit is referred to as "the second blessing." Sometimes a new Christian will ask, "What is the Holy Spirit?"

Perhaps it would be more accurate to ask, *"Who* is the Holy Spirit?" for we have been assured that the Spirit of God is the third person of the Trinity, a part of the Godhead, with all the attributes that can be ascribed to God the Father and God the Son.

It has been said that the Old Testament could be considered the era of the Father; the Gospels, the era of the Son; and from Pentecost forward, the era of the Holy Spirit. Or, to put it another way, after Pente-

cost came the era of prophecy, of fulfill-
ment, and of the Spirit. Every reference to
the Spirit, and there are ninety in the Old
Testament and 260 in the New, is by means
of a personal pronoun.

Why do we know so little of the Holy
Spirit?

Perhaps we have trouble understanding the nature of the Holy Spirit because
we have a different understanding of the
word *ghost*. Perhaps we simply live in too
secular a world. We have become so mate-
rialistic and scientific that we no longer can
think in terms of the spiritual world. Indeed,
some skeptics point out that such a notion
is supernatural, yet we have no trouble ac-
cepting "Close Encounters of the Third
Kind" or "Star Trek" or "Star Wars." Why,
then, is it so difficult to reorient ourselves
to the spiritual world?

Maybe another reason we have diffi-
culty understanding the "indwelling of the
Holy Spirit" is that we confuse the mission
of the Spirit with the mission of Jesus Christ.

Consider Jesus' mission. "Have I been
so long with you and you have not known
the Father? The Father and I are one. I have
come to reveal the Father," Jesus said. Jesus'

mission on earth was to reveal the nature of God the Father to a lost and dying world.

What was the purpose or the mission of the Holy Spirit? To reveal Jesus. B. H. Carroll, founder of Southwestern Seminary, called the Spirit "the Other Jesus." Marcus Dodd referred to him as Jesus' alter ego or other self.

> When he, the Spirit of truth, is come, he will guide you into all truth: for he shall not speak of himself; but whatsoever he shall hear, that shall he speak: and he will shew you things to come. He shall glorify me: for he shall receive of mine, and shall shew it unto you (John 16:13-14).

Jesus promised that he would not leave his followers comfortless, but would send a Comforter to be with them after his departure.

God sent the Son; the Son sent the Spirit. Resist the Spirit, and there is no one else to come!

The Spirit Reproves

What was the role of the Spirit in coming?

When he is come, he will reprove the
world of sin, and of righteousness,
and of judgment: Of sin, because they
believe not on me; of righteousness,
because I go to my Father, and ye see
me no more; of judgment, because the
prince of this world is judged (John
16:8-11).

The word *reprove* means to demon-
strate by argument, convince by presenting
reasons. First, he will convince us of our
sin; then he will convince us of his ability
to save. Why do we believe? Because we
want more than despair; we want the hope
and comfort which the Spirit offers.

Conviction, then, is God's work—not
man's. All we have to do is to present God's
story; he will do the convincing through the
work of the Holy Spirit. And our testimony
is most convincing when we show others
that we, as sinners, have found hope and
comfort in him.

The Spirit Regenerates

The word *regenerate* means to gener-
ate again, to get started anew. An oft-used
phrase is "be born again. (or anew or "from
above")

Apart from regeneration, or rebirth, all men are dead in sin. Without the new birth we have no spiritual life; we experience no change.

But as many as received him, to them gave he power to become the sons of God, even to them that believe on his name: which were born, not of blood, nor of the will of the flesh, nor of the will of man, but of God (John 1:12-13).

"Except a man be born of water and of the Spirit, he cannot enter into the kingdom of God. That which is born of the flesh is flesh; and that which is born of the Spirit is spirit" (John 3:5-6).

Paul made it quite clear what a new birth was like: "Therefore if any man be in Christ, he is a new creature; old things are passed away; behold, all things are become new" (2 Cor. 5:17).

The Spirit Releases

What had the Spirit done for Paul? He tells us in Romans 8:2: "The law of the Spirit of life in Christ Jesus hath made me free from the law of sin and death." What the law could not do, Paul goes on to explain,

the Spirit could do, because to be "spiritually minded is life and peace" (v. 6). Paul
had found bondage in the law; in the Spirit
he found freedom, joy and deliverance.

The Spirit we cannot see, it is true;
but why do we need hope if we can see and
understand everything? The Spirit helps us,
Paul said, by making intercession for us,
even when we are not aware that we need
intercession. The Spirit *releases* us from the
guilt of sin and wins forgiveness for us with
the Almighty.

The Spirit releases to us the strength
needed for daily living—strength to "become mighty" . . . to become as *dynamite*
for the Kingdom of God.

It isn't unusual to hear one say, "I
wish I had lived in the days when Jesus was
alive. I wish I could have seen him face to
face." Or, as one nine-year-old boy put it,
"I wish I had known the *real* Jesus."

The truth is, the real Jesus is with us
now, in the person of the Holy Spirit. Where
Jesus was visible, the Spirit is invisible; but
he is also invincible because he has the
power.

Jesus assured the disciples, "Ye shall
receive power after that the Holy Ghost is
come upon you . . ." (Acts 1:8). From the

very moment of salvation, the Holy Spirit takes up residence in our lives, offering us strength, freedom, power, and comfort.

"Know ye not," asked Paul, "that ye are the temple of God and that the Spirit of God dwelleth in you?"

The Spirit Reassures

When Jesus approached the disciples on the road to Emmaus after his resurrection, he knew he had to reassure them that he would never again leave them alone, that although he must leave them he would not leave them comfortless. The biblical word for the Holy Spirit is "paraclete," or "one who is called alongside," a divine companion.

Phillips Brooks used to conclude his sermons with the words, "The love of God, the peace of Jesus Christ, and the communion of the Holy Spirit be with you always." When there is a bond between the members of the church, believer with believer, and between the members and God, then there is communion. That spirit of fellowship is the work of the Holy Ghost, the divine companion.

The Holy Spirit is all the Father and Son are; he also has attributes of emotion, intellect, and will. But he searches our hearts, he reproves us, he teaches, he comforts, he liberates, he intercedes, he empowers—if we let him.

Big "Doc" Davis, a revered teacher of Greek many years ago in one of our seminaries, was a giant of a man, both physically and spiritually. One day as he stood before the class lecturing, he paused, searching for the right words to convey the meaning of the Greek. In the middle of his explanation, he turned to the class and said, "Young men, I can teach you the meaning of the Greek, but only the Holy Spirit can make the words live in your life."

The indwelling of the Spirit is possible only if we allow him in.

PRAYER

Father, we pray that your Spirit will enter our lives to convict, teach, empower, and comfort us. We plead for the wind and the fire of your words and your love to be demonstrated in us. Amen.

11 *Because of His Assurance*

(John 3:16-18, 5:24, 10:1-2, 25-30; Colossians 3:1-3; Hebrews 6:4-6)

> For I am persuaded, that neither death, nor life . . . shall be able to separate us from the love of God (Romans 8:38-39).

One of the most difficult doctrines in the New Testament is the doctrine of "once saved, always saved." That phrase has long been a theological battleground in evangelical denominations.

Perhaps we need a new way of talking about this doctrine. Maybe we could refer to it as the "assurance or the security of the saved," because there is a difference. Everyone who is a Christian has the security of the believer, but all who are saved do not have the assurance of their salvation.

Why is that? you ask. Why do we not feel assured of our salvation? Most people believe that we are debating the wrong issue—that the question is not whether we are once saved, always saved, but rather whether we are saved today and lost tomor-

row! But why tomorrow? If we feel that
way—that people can never escape sin—
then why not "saved today, lost today," because the opportunity for sin is as present
today as tomorrow?

The point is that, although we are
never free of the presence of sin, we *are*—
through faith in Jesus Christ—free of the
penalty of sin.

To what degree does a person have
to sin to be lost? And what *is* sin? To many,
a sinner is someone they don't like doing
something they would like to do but don't.
To some, sin is the use of cosmetics. To others it is tobacco, and to still others it is mixed
swimming. Sin is not the same in Florida
as it is in Texas or California.

Only one thing is sure. The only time
a person starts being free of sin is when he
is saved, when Jesus has come into his heart
and offered freedom and grace.

I do not believe in the doctrine of
apostasy or "falling from grace." I do not
believe the Bible teaches that. I do believe
that the Bible teaches the security of the
believer. Not the security of the church
member, however—that is a separate issue,
although it ought not be.

The eternal security of the believer

is sometimes called the "perseverance of the saints," but to express it that way puts the emphasis on the "saint" or the individual. It may be the individual who perseveres, but it is God who *preserves.*

I would not be alive today were it not for a man who held onto me while I was drowning—held on long after I had turned loose. In the same way, God preserves, long after we have ceased to persevere. He holds on, even when we falter and let go.

How is this possible?

Sovereignty (Col. 3:3)

"Your life is hid with Christ in God." So says Paul in his letter to the Colossians. We are assured of God's continuing presence because he is sovereign. He is the Good Shepherd, and we the sheep know his voice. The sovereign voice speaks in John 10:28-29:

> I give unto them eternal life; and they shall never perish, neither shall any man pluck them out of my hand. My Father, which gave them me, is greater than all; and no man is able to pluck them out of my Father's hand.

Can there be any greater security than that? than to be in the hands of God? "He that keepeth thee will not slumber," says the psalmist (121:3).

How can sin conquer if God cast out Satan? Did not Satan admit that he was powerless with Job and that for all the distress and misery which Satan caused Job, Job's faith in God was still strong? Satan moaned, "Thou hast hedged him about."

We are his property, and he has promised us eternal life. Would God select, or elect, us and then neglect his children? The young child adopted by a loving family told her new brother, "I'm your *picked* baby." Would a "picked child" of God be neglected any more than a longed-for orphan who has found a new home?

But you are talking about God's act of holding on, you say, not man's. True, because our hope is built on "nothing less than Jesus' blood and righteousness." Christ is our solid rock. We will not be left to ourselves.

Salvation (Eph. 2:8-9)

Another doctrine which has long been debated in the church is that of faith versus works. Many who teach salvation by grace do not appear to believe it, as they emphasize the importance of works "to *keep* saved." In Ephesians Paul says clearly:

> For by grace are ye saved through faith; and that not of yourselves: it is the gift of God: not of works, lest any man should boast" (2:8-9).

Salvation comes to persons only by the unmerited favor of God. It cannot be earned or bought at any price. It costs nothing. Salvation is free. Salvation is God's gift to the believer, to the lost.

Rewards are God's gift to the saved, for works done in the flesh. It is possible to lose one's rewards; it is not possible to lose one's salvation. "If any man's work shall be burned, he shall suffer loss: but he himself shall be saved" (1 Cor. 3:15). This verse should not be interpreted as a license to sin, though, because the believer wants to please God.

Sonship (John 1:12)

"Behold, what manner of love the father hast bestowed on us," wrote John, "that we should be called the sons of God" (1 John 3:1). What love, indeed!

The only cost of being a child of God's

family is that we be believers: "But as many
as received him, to them gave he power to
become the sons of God, even to them that
believe on his name" (John 1:12). *All* men,
whether Jew or Gentile, were offered the
gift of salvation. The gift is theirs to accept
or reject. To accept means immediate salvation and eternal life. How can one say no?

The Scriptures do not teach that every
church member is saved. Look at Judas! He
was one of the select twelve, and he was
unfaithful. The percentage isn't any better
today.

Nor does the Bible teach that refor-
mation is the same as regeneration.

Or that profess-ors are the same as
possess-ors.

The fellowship of our sonship can be
broken, but not our relationship with God.

First Peter 1:3-5 tells us we are "begotten of God," and what God begets (or gives
birth to) he doesn't forget.

Blessed be the God and Father of our
Lord Jesus Christ, which according
to his abundant mercy hath begotten
us again unto a lively hope by the resurrection of Jesus Christ from the
dead, to an inheritance incorruptible,

and undefiled, and that fadeth not
away, reserved in heaven for you,
who are kept by the power of God
through faith unto salvation ready to
be revealed in the last time.

"To an inheritance . . . that fadeth
not away," the apostle writes.

A father once called his children together and confessed, "At one time I had
an inheritance for you, but it is gone now.
I have spent it on bad decisions."

Your heavenly Father will not waste
your inheritance. It is safe with him. "I
know whom I have believed," wrote Paul,
"and am persuaded that he is able to keep
that which I've committed unto him against
that day."

As sons of God, we have a forgiven
past, a fearless present, and fine prospects
for the future. If you leave the words "ever-
lasting life" out of John 3:16, all you have
is an incomplete sentence.

We cannot conceive what God has
prepared for us. What more beautiful promise could we have than that of Romans 8?

Who shall separate us from the love
of Christ? shall tribulation, or distress, or persecution, or famine, or

nakedness, or peril, or sword? . . .
Nay, in all these things we are more
than conquerors through him that
loved us. For I am persuaded, that
neither death, nor life, nor angels,
nor principalities, nor powers, nor
things present, nor things to come,
nor height, nor depth, nor any other
creature, shall be able to separate us
from the love of God, which is in
Christ Jesus our Lord (vv. 35,37-39).

PRAYER

Father, the words of Paul express better than we are able the confidence we have
in our salvation through Jesus Christ.
Amen.

12 Because of His Overcoming

(Romans 8:37, John 16:33, 1 John 5:4)

> I have overcome the world (John 16:33).

Some words become obsolete and meaningless with the passage of time. Others change their meaning through the centuries. Others, though, retain their meaning. One of those is the word victory. The unchanged word rings with clarity and pungency; it is easily understood in most languages. In its truest sense, it is one of the most stimulating words in any language.

To the line soldier, victory means driving back the enemy. To the Christian the meaning is essentially the same: divine deliverance! The enemy has been driven back and conquered!

Jesus' declaration was neither a prediction nor a prophecy—it was a statement of fact. "Be of good cheer; I have overcome the world." Victory is already accomplished.

This is an unusual statement in view of the fact that Jesus was awaiting the footsteps of the Roman soldiers in the garden of Gethsemane . . .

. . . in view of the fact that one of the twelve, Judas Iscariot, had just sold out Jesus for thirty pieces of silver . . .

. . . in view of the fact that Christ was facing the cross and the tomb.

Here was a man left with only eleven friends at the end, eleven out of the many who had followed him and listened to his messages.

As John recorded the words of Jesus, several decades after the event, he still recalled the encouragement Jesus offered those who remained. He told the world: "Whatsoever is born of God overcometh the world . . . even our faith" (1 John 5:4). Rome may have put his feet on Patmos, he declared, but God had set his heart in heaven. Like John, all those who believe are conquerors through faith in Jesus Christ.

The Conflicts of Battle!

Without conflict there is no quest.
Without battle there is no victory.
Without sweat there are no sweets.
Without a cross there is no crown.

The early Christians knew this by heart and by personal experience. To become a Christian was to become a soldier.

Too much of our preaching today plays down this fundamental truth. We forget too easily that all through the New Testament we are challenged to "endure hardness as a soldier of the Lord Jesus." We are told to "put on the whole armour of God," for we do not wrestle with things of this world, but against principalities and powers of evil.

The early Christians knew well that at any time, because of their loyalty and love for God, they might be separated from their families by nakedness or peril or sword. But Paul assured them that nothing can separate them from the love of God.

Christianity is more than a "joy ride." To be sure, a Christian will experience considerable joy in his new life. But an ongoing emotional "high," a "mountaintop experience," is not the essence of Christianity any more than it is the essence of living. Most of life is spent dealing with the routine, the everyday. Christianity also sinks into routine, dips into the difficult areas of life, requires that we take up our cross and deny ourselves. The battles of self-denial improve the quality of the soldiers in Gideon's army.

We must recognize that the conflicts of life are conflicts between Satan and the Savior, between righteousness and unrighteousness, between the forces of this world and the power of God. Jesus never painted the scene with false colors. He reduced the number of his followers from hundreds to a handful. Now, as then, the noise of battle will frighten the timid souls, but a core of good, strong fighters will be victorious.

The Conquest of Trials!

In the third century A.D., the Bishop of Carthage wrote:

If I could go yonder to the highest hill, if I could stand and look down on the world from afar, I would see the Roman soldiers on the main highways as they batter down the weak nations of the world. I would look yonder and see the pirates as they sail the seven seas. Yonder I would see bribery, and yonder, nothing but spoils and laughter and things of ill repute. And I would find a people, a people rejected and lowly and despised of men. And I would see these people as victorious, people who have overcome the world and conquered self, people who are victors in Christ, who can say with Paul, "Nay, in all these things we are more than conquerors through him who loved us."

Jesus walked the earth in human form, was tempted as men are tempted, was beset with human problems, was forced to meet Satan with a hungry heart and a saddened soul. But he met him with the Word of God and was victorious.

Sometimes victories in battle are empty because of the losses. To win a battle that is so costly is to win an empty (Pyrrhic) victory. But Paul tells us that our battles are easily won when we hold onto the Lord. Our weapon of warfare is our assurance of faith. After all, there is a vast difference between going into battle surrounded by your enemies and without weapons or resources, and going into battle with the promise of aid.

Samson forgot the source of his power. The source of our power is not in our feet, for the "Hound of Heaven" can outrun us. It is not in our hands, for Satan is stronger. It is not in our minds, for the fiend is more clever than we. Our strength is in our ideals. We will triumph when we become equal to the faith and spirit in us and recognize that we have a partner in the presence of God.

Samson was able to wrestle with his own hands and overpower the lion. He was able to destroy countless men. But when he forgot the source of his strength, the power of God went out from him, and he was blinded, bound, and tied to a milling wheel, despised and rejected by men. Ultimately Samson was taken to the pagan temple, where he prayed the prayer of a backslider and brought down the temple on the wicked.

One more time, Samson begged, one more time! The late Dr. Robert G. Lee tells of being met in the hallway outside the sanctuary of his church by a man destroyed by the ravages of disease and a sinful life. Dr. Lee no longer recognized the man he had once known so well, so different did he look. "Robert," the man said, addressing the minister by his first name, "I am going to die soon. I have slipped out of the hospital tonight because you are the only preacher friend I have left. Please, please, let me preach one more time. I have so much to say."

It was far sadder, Dr. Lee said, to walk away at that moment from a man who was already dead than it was to walk away from his grave one week later.

Take heed lest you stumble, for the trials and battles you face are real and not imaginary. Yet, take comfort in the fact that the aid of the Lord is real, and he will sustain you in battle if you believe on him.

"Nay, we are more than conquerors through him who loved us."

Communication of Victory!

A minister who had recently lost his wife took his seven-year-old daughter with him to Europe. They were crossing the ocean on a ship, and one of the passengers learned that he was a minister. The Captain came to him and asked if he would conduct the Sunday services. "I do not know what denomination you are," the Captain said, "but I wish you would speak on the love of God."

This was a difficult topic for the minister, who was still deep in grief over the loss of his wife. But because he had survived this test of his faith, he was able to stand before the people and talk about the immeasurable love of Christ.

After lunch he and his daughter were standing on deck, leaning on the railing. The little girl said, "Daddy, you said that God loves us. How much does he love us?"

"More than anybody," said the father.

"Daddy, does God love us as much as Mommy loved us?"

The father answered yes, then looked out over the ocean. He said, "Look. Look in that direction. God's love extends farther than that." Pointing in the opposite direction over endless miles of ocean, he said, "Look the other way. God's love is greater than that." Pointing at the sky he said, "God's love is taller than that," and down at the ocean, "God's love is deeper than that."

Biting her lip to hold back the tears, the little girl said, "Daddy, isn't it wonderful that we are standing out here in the middle of it?"

Despite the darkness of battle, we have the assurance that we are standing in the middle of God's love. Thanks be to God for the victory that is ours through our Lord Jesus Christ.

PRAYER

Yours is the glory, Father, for you have done great things. Help us to recognize that life—the Christian life—is a battle we can win because you love us. Help us to communicate the victory that is ours. Amen.

13   Because of His Hereafter

(Matthew 10:28; John 11:25-26)

> Whosoever liveth and believeth in
> me shall never die (John 11:26).

Death has been different since Jesus came. Before him, men felt they were born only to live. But Jesus was unique; he was born for only one reason, and that was to die. However, with death came resurrection and this assurance from the Savior: "I am the resurrection, and the life: he that believeth in me, though he were dead, yet shall he live" (John 11:25).

The thought of death is painful to all of us. Yet it would be far more painful if we did not discuss it openly and try to come to grips with it. Customs have changed. Funeral homes once decorated in black or brown are now trimmed in pastel colors. But it is still death to die, and the true color of death will be determined largely by our choices in this life.

Most of us have asked ourselves at some time, "Where am I going? What are my goals? What will be my lot in life? Where did I come from?" Most of these questions have to do with our choices concerning vocation, marriage partner, whether to have children, and the like.

But Jesus, asking the same questions, wanted to know where we are going spiritually. He knew that our destiny after life would be determined by our choices in this life.

Jesus warned that we would wrestle with many enemies in this life, but that in the end we would face the last and greatest enemy, the final one. As someone said, "If the sweetest word in our language is *mother,* the saddest word is *sin,* the harshest word is *no,* the weakest word is *if,* God's favorite word is *come,* then surely we could say that the inevitable word for man is *death."* Death will not be denied.

Death is not a concept we face easily. We avoid using the word at all. We speak of friends "passing away." We say *"if* I die" instead of *"when* I die." We stand in awe and fear of the mystery of death, a mystery unsolved by science, technology, or the occult.

Try as we might, we do not understand either the beginning or the end of life, and we can identify with Dr. Temple who wrote, "For myself, I do cling to it [life after death] immensely. I do not mean that I want it for myself as a mere continuance, but I want it for my understanding of life."

Truly, life has no meaning without Job's question and Jesus' answer.

Finality of Death

A group of college students was asked if they would want to be told if death were imminent. More than 50 percent said they would not. Still, an evasive attitude will no more protect you from the fact of death than the sand will hide the ostrich. W. R. Hearst banished the use of the word *death* on his estate, but he could not banish the fact of death from his life.

The idea of death is presented for the first time in Genesis, where life is first conceived: "And the Lord God formed man of the dust of the ground, and breathed into his nostrils the breath of life; and man became a living soul" (2:7). A few verses later, when Adam and Eve have eaten of the forbidden fruit, we hear:

In the sweat of thy face shalt thou
eat bread, till thou return unto the
ground; for out of it wast thou taken:
for dust thou art, and unto dust shalt
thou return (3:19).

When Adam chose disobedience and sin, he
chose spiritual death, even though he was
not to die physically for 930 more years.

We come face to face with physical
death in the Old Testament when Cain slays
Abel. Since that moment, death has stalked
the human race—not a phantom or a dream,
but a definite separation of soul from body.

Death will terminate our earthly
plans. "Boast thyself not of tomorrow," for
death will take you unawares. Prepare!

Death will terminate our earthly bod-
ies, and corruption will put on incorruption.
But Jesus said, "Fear not them which kill
the body, but are not able to kill the soul:
but rather fear him which is able to destroy
both soul and body in hell" (Matt. 10:28).

Death will terminate our day of grace,
for if we are without belief, between God
and us "there is a great gulf fixed."

How do you explain to a friend, a
loved one, a relative, an acquaintance, a
church member, the answer to the question

why? Why me? Why my family? Why do we suffer this way? Why are we left in this pain, without joy and without hope? These are questions for which there is no answer, questions that tear your heart out. Our only hope is Jesus' assurance that, beyond physical death, there is life, eternal life.

Reality of Hell

We must now take a look at the most ignored, most stubbornly persistent doctrine in the Bible. Hell is mentioned 234 times in the New Testament, ten times as many as heaven! Yet heaven is always in season, while there never seems to be an appropriate time to discuss hell.

Does this mean that the fires of hell are burning less brightly, that they are only smoldering, and that all we have left is the ashes? In some churches hell hasn't been a sermon topic for forty years. Is this a compliment or an indictment? I know that our audiences are modern, that we live in the 1970s when sin is unfashionable and hell is an antiquated notion. But sin and hell exist; Jesus himself was the world's greatest authority on the subject.

Remember his description of the rich man in hell talking to Lazarus in heaven?

If men have not heard the voices of Moses and the prophets, said Jesus, they will pay no attention to the warnings of a dead man in hell! It is possible for intellectualism to laugh hell out of the pulpit, but it is not possible to laugh it out of the Bible.

"The fool hath said in his heart, There is no God" (Ps. 14:1). Wasn't Noah the only man who believed the flood would come? Weren't Abraham and Lot the only ones who believed Sodom and Gomorrah would be destroyed?

True, hell is horrible, but so are war, disease, death, and decay. Hell was not prepared for the souls of persons, but for the devil and his angels. People must *choose* it!

No, hell will never be a popular doctrine. It will always be misunderstood, and it will usually be controversial. But whatever it is, it can never be reduced simply to profanity or a joke.

Sublimity of Heaven

An old black spiritual goes, "Everybody talkin' 'bout heaven ain't a-goin' there." In the words of Jesus, "Not everyone that saith unto me, Lord, Lord, shall enter the kingdom of heaven."

Paul found heaven sublime. Even counting all that is good and precious in this life, he still felt that "to die is gain."

Heaven is no more an illusion than is hell. It is not the sleep of the saints or the figment of a hopeful imagination. Heaven is real. "If I go," Jesus promised, "I go to prepare a place for you, and I will come again and receive you there, that where I am, there you may be also." "Eye hath not seen, nor ear heard, neither have entered into the heart of man, the things which God hath prepared for them that love him" (1 Cor. 2:9). A land of promise, a blessed end, a home, sweet home. That is what awaits the believer at the end of his journey. Room, reward, reunion, release, and recognition!

Some years ago a minister commented cynically that the world is no longer interested in "a land that is fairer than day," but only in a world where there are two cars in every garage, a set of golf clubs in the country club locker, a steak on every grill, a TV in every room, and a bankroll in every pocket. That may be so, but whether we are interested or not at this moment, the day will come when we must face the urgent questions of life, and our interest will be rekindled.

Will we know each other in heaven? The disciples recognized Moses and Elijah

on the mount of transfiguration. We have
not been told that we will not know our
loved ones—only that we will not be the
same then as we are now. "We shall know,
even as we are known," wrote Paul. If we
"see through a glass darkly" now, then we
shall see "face to face."

Jesus is preparing a place. His Word
teaches us: "I have set before thee life and
death; therefore, choose life!" If he didn't
tell us more about heaven, perhaps it is because he knew we wouldn't believe it. Or
perhaps he wanted to *show* us.

What can the Christian say about
death? Not much. But the Christian can say
much *to* death: "O death, where is thy sting?
O grave, where is thy victory?" For we are
more than conquerors in Christ—over sorrow, loneliness, life, and death.

PRAYER

Our Father, help us to remember,
while we look forward to our heavenly
home, that heaven is under our feet as well
as over our heads. May we recognize that
we have a life to live while we are here,
and that how we live here will have much
to do with how we live hereafter. Amen.